NIGHT VISION

To: Johnny,

For connections over the years
and for shared heritage

-Kendel

May 3rd, 2014

ALSO BY KENDEL HIPPOLYTE

Island in the Sun — Side 2
Bearings
The Labyrinth
Birthright
Fault Lines

KENDEL HIPPOLYTE

NIGHT VISION

PEEPAL TREE

First published in the USA
TriQuarterly Books
Northwestern University Press 2005.
This edition published in Great Britain in 2014
Peepal Tree Press Ltd
17 King's Avenue
Leeds LS6 1QS
UK

ISBN 13: 9781845232351

Supported by
ARTS COUNCIL
ENGLAND

CONTENTS

NOT MADE WITH HANDS
For Pat Turnbull

These housing blocks that now squat
next to the marsh that was the town's botanical gardens
were set up by the bureau's technocrats to dam the oozing crawl
of rank-smell slum over the city's urbane surface.
These prefabricated structures, straight edged, right angled
for those who can afford, were designed to rise three stories high
above the living standard of those turbulent, foulmouthed generations
of fishermen's grandchildren everyone calls Conway people.

In the blueprint vision of the bureau
these low-rise schemes would elevate – and, if not, eliminate
(from sight, of course) – the poor,
raise them above or raze them from
their stink-drain squalor, their brawling quarrelling over whose man or woman
fock whose man or woman, who pelt stone, who slash who
wid who blade, who buy, who sell, who t'ief
what from who, for what, and who responsible
for all dis rassclaat, bumbabloodclaat mixup mixup
dat somebody somewhere fixup and want to tell us dis is life!
The prefabs were to block all that.
In the bureau's diagrams and flowcharts,
after the eliminations (i.e. redesignations, relocations),
whatever, if any, of these sprawling lives were left
had to be framed within the pre-stressed concrete flats,
hoisted and slabbed each one into its place,
fitted into the structure of the overall design.
That's why in the bureau's plan
there are no zigzag alleys, ribboning child roads,
shortcuts that hello past a back door,
or any of these unnamed weeds and half-wild flowers,
the ones that always spring up after you have stepped on them,
almost unnoticed usually, taken as natural,
like the uncounted, unaccountable acts of grace
that Conway people scattered easily among curses and quarrelling

and that took root, growing in common ground,
and that created, despite everything, a cultivation of community.

The bureau, in its plan, statistically edged all of that
outside the margin, outside the strict cost-benefit calculation,
as slight intangibles too vague to be concretized
and better ruled out.
And so today, a hot, flat, featureless, square afternoon
a year after the stamped approval of the blueprint,
two of the few Conway mothers lucky and hustling enough
to manage finally to fit themselves into the dead lines
stare – across the bare asphalt quadrangle –
at the closed ranks of doors and windows opposite,
where their unnamed middle-incoming neighbours live, or at least reside.
Mildred, talking to Belle about the year before –
of the bulldozers, houses breaking, people leaving the condemned homes
and ways of generations – *and i not saying*
dat to live wid rat and rubbish is a better t'ing.
But – and i will say it simple so no one misunderstands –
somet'ing missing. And look like is we go have to find,
somehow, a way to build again somet'ing dat we did leave behind,
de other kinda house, not made wid hands.

CITY

Watching this city, like a relative that i have grown estranged from,
hobbling up the hillsides, at first on the wooden crutches of small houses,
then higher up, on Zimmer frames of the more well-appointed residences,

i see no way for us to be together as we were before… before what?
Can't even find the words, far less a place to meet we can agree on.
Once we could meet here, at the centre, where all i know and love began,

but it's where all are fleeing from – too congested, stinking, full of noises.
All the ways there are choked; the viscous, spastic flow of commercial traffic
clogs the arteries to the city's heart and it becomes, slowly, sclerotic.

Each month new cheap boutiques open, have sales, shut down, re-open
in houses that you once knew clattering with children, ruled by raucous mothers.
The signs show our times: FOXY, HIJACK. Next month there'll be others.

Daytime, the whole scene jumps like crackling coloured popcorn; it's at night
you feel what's gone – family sounds, fussing, food smells, kids running wild.
How can you walk a whole block and not hear even one child?

If houses are real only through people living in them, if roofs are held up
by hands, not rafters, i see why i do not recognize these places in the sun's glare,
yet at night, passing, i can hear whispers of those no longer there.

But who has made it so? If the oil slick of commerce, spreading, has seeped
through to the centre till the ones who live there have to move,
why is this? What happens to a heartland when the original dwellers leave?

And what happens to what used to be the hinterland, the country?
I am imagining houses, split-level bungalows and shacks, metastasizing
out of green earth, hills hardening into a mass of lurid scabs, erasing

certain sounds, textures, the flight and call and scurrying and scent
of nature waking, sleeping, in work and dream toward a spiralling destiny
we can no longer hear, perhaps no longer are a part of, finally.

Why is all this? And why, again, this helpless anger at the question?
And then that wry acknowledgment, late each time although i try,
that it is not the anger which is helpless – I know – it is i.

Because i am the city. So are you. We are a confused, stinking place.
It is my centre, your heart that our lives have polluted, our lies have choked;
it is the ways of the Imagination that we first so casually blocked.

The city shows us who we are, that's all. Running from it, we meet
our selves in virulent replication. Escape is not possible, only transformation.
Only a healing that must start here, at the centre, where it all began.

42 CHISEL STREET

42 Chisel Street. The house, like most, is gone. A beauty salon now,
where fluttering girls can make the dullest hair bounce, curl, and glisten.

Listen

"Who's that?" i look around. Not a sound now, and yet
something else moves in the blue late night, small and shy. i hear:

Here

"Where? Where are you? i can't see. Who are you? Tell me, who?
Who is this calling out to me? And why?"

I

"You sound familiar. You grew up in this place? Show me your face once,
and i'll remember. Is it because you think i will not know?"

No

"Then show me. If you were one of us, give me your trust now
and tell me who you are so our conversation can continue."

You

"What do you mean? That you are me? Last son of Geraldine and Kent?
Brother of Kent Jr. and Hogarth? A grandmother who'd lived in Cayenne?"

Ken

"When we left this place, i was just nine. Did i leave you behind here?
And is this where you live? And is your life ongoing?"

Going

"Like so much else. Both new and old. We don't know what to hold on to
anymore. We don't know what we should believe."

Leave

"You stayed. 42 Chisel Street. Did you wait forty years to meet me here
again? i walked by so often, blind. What can i do to amend?"

End

"i am a poet now i remember you liked rhymes. But, Kendel, sometimes, honestly, i wonder: What can poetry and poets do with so much passing?"

Sing

sing

KINKY BLUES

in the city out here, i'm drowning in my weird
from trying to stay real
head floating, body going under
head sailing, but i'm going under

the women sell plums, the men sell chocolate bars
buy one or the other or both
but watch your buying, some are rotten already
money is precious and rot spreads too easy

up at the crossroads, i'm selling my face
but no one's buying – who needs a face
i pocket my face, put on a blank
too late for faces, i put on a blank

last night dark as asphalt, my headlight blew out
now i finally know where i'm going
looking for kinky, he's changed his address
still the same place, but he's changed his address

living out my afraid, i'm dying in my alive
i must learn to sing out of key
feels strange at first, but i'll soon be alright
soon's i learn this song, i'll be alright

CITY GRAFFITI

so my city,
in your half-assed state,
what should you do?
perhaps emigrate?

       strict geometry of streets
       stolid arithmetical sum of citizens
       twisted algebra of xy formula bureaucrats
       right-angled rigid rule of set square men
       only the river loops and wonders
       but it doesn't count

CITY VOICES

I. Beck

One time in school i set a high jump record. Up to that time
no one so young had ever jump so high.
And from that time, i wanted to go higher.
Lemme tell you,
when you leave ground, going to meet the bar,
you lifting up your whole life with you,
and then it have a moment when you light, just light,
and all you see is sky.
Everyone thought i woulda make it – with my subjects, good job, girlfriend.
But somehow all that was just a bar.
i wanted to go higher.
And look, i tell no lie, the first few times
was like the day i set the record:
rush of air, i leaving ground, i looking only up, the sky,
my life light, drifting like a cloud.
Is after the first few times that everything get heavy.
As each thing drop out of me life – job, girlfriend, big ambition –
i replace it with a rock,
and my life get heavier, harder to lift up from the ground.
But then the other things i didn't know that i was carrying
started to drop off too and by themselves:
false pride – 'cause now i washing car and begging;
false friend – i didn't know i had so many;
the emperor clothes of social status – my whole life bareback now;
the beam from my own eye – all that drop and i get light.
Things start to clear.
One day, on a street corner opposite a bank,
i stand up praying with a brethren for the strength
to leave the cold hard rock i on too long
and leap up to the Rock that is higher than i.
So when that hot quick-trigger-finger Babylon arrest i
after that stupid quarrel with that woman,
i couldn't believe i fall so low. i coulda cry.

15

Like i throw down the bar again.
i? Who just start seeing how to rise above my life?
Just measuring the distance, checking my strength for all i'll have to do?
Not i! i break 'way. i start to run.
And as i running, I see my whole life clear,
and not mine only, everybody own, the whole society.
I see the bar that there in front each one of we.
And i look up, blue sky, right leg starting to lift,
then I hear someone cry; I look down.
Someone bleeding on the ground: not I.
I gone clear.

2. Cool Blood

All dat di'n' need to happen. i set up a plan.
Mark him. Let dem see.
Good plan, but dem bwoy fock it up.
Too excited. Once dem bust blood
dem wild out.
Blood is a t'ing you have to use.
                    My blood cool.
Dem always say dat – like is somet'ing so bad.
Fock dat. i say you have a plan, stay wid it.
Always. Could be a baby dat you goin' to kill,
still have a plan.
Wha' i set up was simple:
slash our X four place –
forehead, nose, one on each cheek –
he cyah hide everyt'ing.
Let dem other AK-47 jesterer bwoy see
is we run t'ings.
Four little X, dis whole t'ing woulda settle.
But Jerome. Once dat man see blood –
wild.
Wha' he expec'? De man go take four X

without a fight, a scream?
One X alone i have time put, forehead –
de AK fling Jerome off, bite Chaga hand,
and try to run. But i done stick de knife already
in his leg. Jerome di'n' have to burn him.
Is de blood. It get him hot. Forget de plan.
So look now – a whole round
just to kill Jerome, 'cause my blade, you know...
And since Jerome blaze de man out
we still eh have no warning to de AK posse.
Today i have to get another one.
But dis time i go do de whole t'ing
me one, in cool blood.

3. *Talk*

Girl, i shoulda know somet'ing was different
that time.
He akse me my name and i tell him.
i does never tell dem my name, my real name.
i does say Foxy or Ebony or June,
somet'ing stupidee or simple like that.
But he akse like he really want to know,
and just so
my real name fly out.
He say he only want to talk.
Well, in my mind, i put a f
where he did have a t.
i figure he's one of de shy ones –
doh want to come straight, does have to play li'l bit –
and sometimes i doh mind dat, sometimes it does be nice.
And anyway, he paying, so...
But all like how he quiet and shy, i check
i have to take de lead.
So when we reach de room –

17

and i smiling, remembering how he say "talk" –
i say: "So you want you and me to fock
until i scream?"
He say: "No. Talk."
And i t'ink: Talk until i scream? Then i ketch meself.
"You want it quiet? Sof'? Slow?"
i start to peel off, one by one.
Maybe if i show some skin – and t'ing, you know?
He let me finish, look me up and down. He say:
"You're beautiful. Let's talk."
i t'inking: But dat is one funny man, yes – wait!
Maybe he funny?
Girl, i try. But all how i t'row me corn
dat cock refuse to crow.
So
i start to talk.
i tell him – i won't say everyt'ing, but
t'ings i t'ink twice to tell a soul, even my own soul,
much less a stranger.
i tell him 'bout de first time, 'bout Harvey,
'bout de pregnancy, de put-out, living by me two young auntie,
'bout how eventually they couldn't keep from me
how they live – like Dawn does say – by de sweat of their pussy
and, though they wasn't happy, i make dem introduce me
'cause you know me and dependency.
But strange, all de time i talking, somet'ing –
starting in me belly – spreading through me, like a t'rill.
And he doh say much, jus' listening, but each time
he touch me wid a question,
he bringing on another fluttering, and i startling each time.
It did strange, but sweet, like… maybe sweeter than dat.
i feel light, somet'ing inside me was lightening.
Then he akse about de baby.
And de lightness and de sweetness dat was spreading stop.
And i feel my throat tighten, like a hand, around de scream.
i tell de man: "He born strange… i cyah talk 'bout dat:"
After dat, i couldn't talk no more. i woulda scream.

De man see dat. He stop. Look straight in me eyes.
Girl, naked is we business, i suppose to know what naked is,
but dat time there, dat moment,
was my first naked.
De man thank me. And then i realize: he going!
i doh know what pass through me,
i feel all kinda t'ing, but mostly vex!
Vex wid de man, vex wid me life,
vex wid da bastard Rodney dat i follow here
for nothing – Trini and Bajan just doh mix –
but vex most wid meself.
And i eh know if so much naked just need company,
or if he just did look too powerful, or if i feel dat he owe me,
but i just hear me self say:
"Where you going? Come! We having sex!
Wha' happen? You sof'?" and grab he crotch.
Everyt'ing was there. Ready. Except the way
he look at me. He call my name.
i jump! 'Cause i had done forget
i'd told him. Then he say: "Bye, songbird."
Songbird? That was his last word.
i never akse his name. He have mine:
Lynette.
Strange, eh? Hardest man i ever met.
But, girl, you okay? You self doh look too right.
Buy you another beer before i go? Dis one done warm.
Yeah, i going. i realize i just decide.
Cyah do dis t'ing.
Tomorrow. Not tonight.

THE HEAD OF MARY RACKLIFFE

The head of Mary Rackliffe
speaks to the man who hacked it from her body:
"You are in hell wherever you are.
Whatever other woman's body you lust after,
undress, fuck, batter, even love,
it will be my face,
my eyes with you forever trapped in them holding the cutlass.
Whatever her shape, her scent,
however her skin whispers under your hands,
when you look up from her breasts, where you have hidden your face,
i will look back at you."

The head of Mary Rackliffe
speaks to the policeman who, that first time, had not listened:
"Listen now. That sound, that slight fleck between each word,
is blood, the drip of blood, on your shoes.
i remember, when i realized you would not hear me,
how i looked down. They were so well polished.
i could see myself. Listen now.
Look down."

The head of Mary Rackliffe
speaks to the women marching in her name and in the name of women:
"It is good. We have always been in marches, always fought,
for others, not our selves. This march must walk another way.
Yet, crossing old boundaries, we will reach
a place no crowd can enter,
where women, loving, sometimes lose themselves, yet find
the true shape and original reason of our humanity –
and it was in that place i loved him.
That place – you do not want to look within as you march past.
But i have lived there. And i want to march with you."

The head of Mary Rackliffe
speaks to the women standing aside, watching the marchers:
"What have you come to see?

20

This severed head, above a gnash of bleeding veins and ganglia,
impaled over a placard? What do you hope to see?
Our steps become uncertain? Gaps in our ranks
where certain women will not touch each other?
Perhaps. We did not ask for saints. Point your stiff fingers
at the adulteress, the mother who steals, the schoolgirl after the abortion.
They are here. So? They are us. And what they are,
their rage and grief and dark, will not become your carnival.
Join these broken lines, or throw the first stone, or,
sisters, go home."

The head of Mary Rackliffe
speaks to the men holding the women they believe they love:
"He loved my body, how it felt to him,
for him. What he hated
was that i saw without him pointing,
i could hear behind his words, i spoke beyond his echo,
i could think.
                    He wanted to separate, like most men,
my body and my mind. This
is the only way. But in that desperate separation,
what fell toward him, what he caught and will forever hold,
was not the body. He saw that, finally.
And do you see
that, trying to sever, in me, thought and feeling,
he believed, somewhere, that he was doing
what you wanted, what all men, always, wanted?
Do you?"

Mary Rackliffe
speaks to the all of us:
"i am less divided now.
If my head and body were joined, if i could live,
it would begin again, the unsleeping struggle to remain whole.
You are as i was, severed:
thought and feeling,   body/mind   woman   man.
You must rejoin your selves, become
one.

21

TEMPLES OF GOV

One hundred steps back from the harboured sea,
which promises every high tide to reclaim its land,
these buildings, wall-eyed, megalithic, stand.

Ministries of government, shrines of official sacrifice,
where priests and acolytes of an unseen power
in cataleptic ritual serve the devourer,

Gov. These monuments rise in his name.
Within, the hierophants, sleeked in sycophancy,
prepare, from our strangled needs, food for the deity.

Within these walls, in corridors and antechambers always, we
wait for a quick signature, a stamp, a word, a one reluctant nod
and each blank, helpless hour is our tribute to the god.

While, on the other side of doors that shut without once opening,
his ministers enact the private rites by which ancestral lands,
homes, lives, within a sleight of handshake, all change hands.

Here the heart's orphan craving for Jerusalem is garroted
at these deaf blocks where children of the heartdream
die bloodlessly, without a scream.

Here are the sanctioned premises of psychic murder.
Here are the halls of bleeding dreams, aborted.
Here toward Formica catafalques walk the unknowing dead.

Temples of Gov – where Ovalea's yearning clear-eyed children
are hacked and sacrificed each day in hecatombs,
so quietly, in air-conditioned rooms.

Temples of Gov – where the dying rule the dead
and the god whose name we do not call,
megalocidal, rules us all.

Temples of Gov – where yet in mutual torturing we hide,
victor and victim, trapped in the ritual because we're terrified,
each one of us, to stop, to walk alone, dark, to our shrine inside.

SNOW

It's snowing in our land.
The warmth evaporates, the cold settles
on hill and house, on friends we knew, on families.
A fallout from a cold war covers them
and they diminish, disappear into a blizzard.
Snow falls, a blitz of words.
News crackles in the air like frostbite,
a bland subtle obliteration hiding from us
the common ground.

Till even flesh and blood numb into snowmen,
caricatures formed with the precipitate from TV screens.
The flakes, the white lies, drift, bury the mindscape,
and we shape our effigies –
"honkies", "terrorists", "reactionaries" –
then smash them.

Snow in the tropics.
Lately we pass each other in a gorge,
fearful between its east and west walls.
We do not call out, we whisper, we dare not declare
that despite this, despite the chilblain hardening over our hearts,
we still are
what we have always been:
Man-Woman, looking for fruitful ground again.

We walk, the flakes fall, wintering the mind,
blurring a dimming memory of garden, shared fruit in warm air.
And we know

by our cold silence, our static fear,
trudging through drift and blur, hoping we'll find our homes again,
we are becoming snow.

GREY

One night, by mistake, they left the TV on.
There'd been a blackout just as the youngest one
was flicking from the Caribbean news to MTV – 34 to 08.
He'd just pressed 0 – then the lights were gone.

What to do? No candles, kerosene lamp, nothing to light.
Thoroughly suburban, no one in the family knew
the full moon stories, the old games; there was no drum.
They switched off everything and said good night.

But they forgot the TV, set to channel 0.
The house remained dark when electricity kicked in,
but the Cyclops's eye flicked open and surveyed the room.
The hiss of static was like someone thinking.

If eyes are, as the ancients tell us, windows to the mind,
there was a mind here whose inmost thought, whose substance,
was a grey void, a zero restless in its turbulence –
visible now after the illusions flickering on other channels.

It had been 3:00 A.M. when the eye first quickened open.
At 3:30, the youngest cried out in his sleep, once,
precisely as it started: the TV's monochrome, electrostatic flux
gusted, convulsed. Then grey flakes drifted from the black box

out into the room. Swarming. Almost soundless. Settling.
A teeming grey undifferentiating scurf filmed over everything.
All separateness of colour, texture, shape gradually blurred.
The swarm stirred, churning softly. Whispered to the next room.

By 5:30, when the mother rose to make the coffee,
the grey had filtered into everything.
She thought that it was overcast, that it was drizzling,
that her arthritis numbed her touch, that she needed more sleep.

It was difficult to understand just what had changed.
Each thing was still there, but the all was different.
Yet from what? If all things were the same
colour, smell, texture, taste, what could be different?

What did the question really even mean, the mother wondered,
her first sip of coffee different too, yet similar –
to what? The way the cup felt?… Her thinking wandered,
words slurred down, whirred to a low hiss, familiar.

It was another family that awoke by 7:00 A.M.
Each sensed it, though no one was sure of why.
No one was sure of anything. The only certainty
was that some difference had made everything the same.

It was in what they ate, an aftertaste of ash;
a furred feel in each touching; was an untraceable whiff
of chloral; a slow haze through which their forms were wavering;
a dragged hush of something distant, pouring. A stuff,

precipitating from a nothing that no one could name,
ghosted the house; things, even gestures, lost their substance,
dissolving to penumbra. The grain and grit of their existence,
loosening, dispersed, faded, slow motion, to a blank frame.

So the house, so the street. Fingers of grey
erased the distinct definitions of what they had lived among,
what they had known, thought they would know for life –
landscape, their neighbours, the shape of each day.

By the week's end, wraiths of it drifting everywhere,
their town, the other towns, the countryside, the country
became glimpses of themselves, tricks of sight and memory,
people flailing through mist for what used to be there.

Month sifted into month. The same, but all had changed.
A sense of irreality became a sediment in every feeling.
The year drained out. It left a people greyer than their years,
left a sense of orphanage, of a whole life estranged.

No one had ever imagined it would come, the dread apocalypse,
so softly. Without thunder, flame. Just ash, day after day
the same, burying everything, the earth transformed into a vague ellipse,
hanging in space, a zero, a blank, drifting blur of grey.

2

A fable? i suppose. But some truths are seen only through fiction.
How else explain our creeping meaninglessness, our sense of stasis,
if not by a miasma seeping to the psyche and becoming, by osmosis,
us? An existential nerve gas that induces slow spiritual annihilation.

Perhaps the air secretes it on those tepid half days
when every business sign fades to a blank, when all doors shut
and buildings gradually subside, dissolving in their shadows,
as cars diminish down an empty street towards a vanishing point.

These afternoons of people who recede from you, from any meaning.
Girl gesturing in a phone booth. Man crossing a bare street.
Images. In an earlier century, they'd have been a pointillist painting.
They're digital now. They move. And yet they do not.

Images. Rewind them. Play. Again. They are no more real
if you try to touch, to listen, to talk to them. The same.
Like the cars and buildings, their substance has become
the odourless grey stuff on the screen no one can feel.

But when did we become so light, so strangered?
What is it that began to fold our words in gauze?
What is that haze, whispering underneath our phrases,
rising through gaps in conversation, obliterating all we said?

It is as though, somewhere in the last century, a Hiroshima of unbelief
blasted the inner being of another generation, elsewhere,
and now its radioactive dust, the nihilistic grey mites of the mind,
is falling on us, and even more on our children, here.

Through the blurring fallout we sometimes vaguely discern
shapes we are not sure of, voices that are ours, yet alien.
Within the grey smog of our uncertainty, something is mutating:
in this brave new world, our first generation of unmeaning.

THE PIPER'S SONG

The piper was nearby:
everyone seemed suddenly restless,
listening; there was
something subtly disturbing
but hard to place. Tension
like when a race was on.
All seemed the same, just that
no one looked you in the face.
Not the children squeaking off to school.
Not the scurrying clerks in the rush hour.
Not the beady-eyed salesmen.
No one. Listening.

They heard it. Rich Yankee-Doodle trill
calling them. They could not be still,
scuttling after the notes. A chase
of creeping bodies, a sneaking swarm swelling into a race
that no one knew the start of, end of, or how to stop
running not to fall, running till someone, going downhill,
asked: "What is this place? Who's the guy with the pipe?
What's he doing? He playing for free? Who's paying?"

They stopped. Dead
quiet for a moment.
Then the melody, more slowly, funeral pace,
wailed long and shrill.

THE PIPER'S CHILDREN

1. Little Boy Blue

Oh where is the boy
who thought people were sheep?
Busy – changing Marx to dollars,
reinterpreting materialism
("This is a new historical context, brother").

He meets you
years after the strike
and hails you – "How's the struggle?" –
just before he ducks into a Mercedes
and leaves you
standing still among the people at the bus stop.

2. Little Tommy Tucker

Little Tommy Tucker
still sings for his supper.
Now what does he eat?
Flesh on a silver platter.
There's a lot of bread
and T knows how to butter.
Just has to play it sweet,
sing to the boss's daughter

that dark dirge in his head:
song of the Pied Piper.

3. Jack Sprat

Jack Sprat
has (so far)
no use for fat.
Muscle, sweat, blood, brain
fuel factories
in various Third Grade countries
for his gain.
His wife
is another matter.
She grows fatter
from each fund-raising banquet,
celebrity junket,
and a daily course of social patter.
Still, they are symbiotic,
fat and lean,
a well-greased machine.
They scoop the bounty
of the crumbling earth
onto a silver platter
and between them both
they lick it clean.

4. Margery
                and
                        Johnny

She saw,
Margery Daw,
just how the game was played.
One went up,
another came down.
To each upgrading,
a downsizing.
In one company, stock rising;

in another, a sudden drop.
Some got it made;
some flop.
And people too: take Johnny —
used to be
upwardly mobile, of course
had all the economic leverage
on his side.
Then, after he reached the top,
things started to slide.
Everything came down:
Dow Jones average
company stock
personal portfolio
salary.
Now the new boss, his CEO,
is Margery.

5. *Aging Playboy on the American economy*

This is how you do it.
During the boom,
minimal investment, quick returns, high turnover.
Later, expect things to sag, interest will drop, etc.
Takes a while for old Dow Jones to rise
to former levels, and the plunge is swift.
Course, you can prolong the boom time,
get an extension — 'specially if you
keep juggling commodities, trading partners,
don't get stuck in one thing for too long.
But yeah, eventually, i guess, devaluation tells.
They say that in real terms —
in real terms, mind you, not fancy statistics;
all those figures, nicely rounded off can fool you —
the actual value's been going down
on everything around for years now.

i can believe that. i've seen it.
i tell you, the economy's a bitch.
Soon you'll need a billion just to
talk anybody into letting you get any
kind of even the most temporary partnership going.
i don't think i should give up, though.
Things with me are slow right now, but
i can sense a boom ahead.
i know. i've got that twitch.
Besides, what's the alternative?
This is what made us great, this
is America.

SALE – A MILLENNIUM RAP

For George Lamming

Everything had to go, there was new stuff to sell
Old stock to dispose of, the century was ending
A last feeding frenzy of getting and spending
Commodities swarming from heaven to hell
Profits on a gargantuan scale
It was the sale of the century
In the century of the sale

There were cereal bowls from the skulls of Cambodia
Fine sculpture from skeletons of Ethiopia
A rush on for shoes, all kinds and all sizes
Limited stocks from the factories of Auschwitz
And the bidding was on for the Holy Grail
In the sale of the century
In the century of the sale

Large assortments of organs, internal, external
New livers, placentas, fresh eyeballs, new hearts
Megagallons of blood, silos full of bone marrow
A brisk one-way trade in used body parts
South to North, East to West, gross and retail
The poor sold themselves
In the century of the sale

Demand and supply ruled the great halls of learning
Data was expensive, wisdom was free
A corporate-sponsored production of knowledge
Intellectual fast food, courtesy of McD
And Oxford and Cambridge and Harvard and Yale
Had been bought by the Colonel
In the century of the sale

Mephistopheles came, offering diamonds and gold
But he couldn't get a taker, all the souls had been sold
They were tied in investments, put in bonds and in stocks
Sealed in a portfolio, locked in a strongbox
Satan offered the whole world – all to no avail
Souls were just a dead loss
In the century of the sale

In previous centuries, death was the great leveller
And birth the beginning of all possibilities
Now death had no currency, a dishonoured cheque
And birth was negotiable, a question of fees
Murder by contract, babies by e-mail
It was one and the same
In the century of the sale

Money literally bought time and time became money
They found ways of converting millennia to millions
So with poor/dead slum children and rich/old patricians
We came to the end of the twentieth century
With history price-labelled, futures for sale
All the joy and the reason of living dried stale
But everything had to go or the market would fail
And now history was screaming a last bitter wail
For mined valleys of dread, acid rains of sly magistery
The grey drifts of anomie, white wastes of the dead
For the ticker tape stuttering its dark lines of profit
For the hopelessness, lovelessness, undying death of it
History was screaming for all that was lost
For the unreckonable, unpayable, unendurable cost
Of a greed so enormous it was cosmic in scale
And had ruled all our lives
In the century of the sale.

NIGHT VISION

1

It's hard to see anything without history.
Days leave their residue, a film over the eyes,
far more the centuries. We see by memory
and the memories of generations become cataracts
occluding the child-clear visioning of Eden.
Because we see with history,
it is difficult to see through it. And yet we must
or we become it, become nothing else but history.

2

But how to see, yet see beyond:
three caravels whose keels severed the horizon line between the worlds,
Columbus's abscessive dreams rupturing, blood on the white sand of centuries
clotting into countries of a new map of the world;
to see beyond:
canoe-eyed warriors women children beautiful as pottery,
their red-earth bodies pitted from insidious arrows of plague,
their glazing eyes holding the dimming stare of their last zemis;
how to see:
the desperate indentured servants, scarecrow tobacco farmers
who'd fled from hungering Ireland, the hardening boundaries of England,
chewed to white trash in the grinding maws of sugar factories;
beyond:
millions of Africans contorted into writhings of black coral on the sea-floor,
and the survivors living the other death, from the first lash of sunlight
till the cool, blessed dark dried out the whip and cutlass
while they unburied, nightly, the still-warm, holy, undying dream.
How
to see yet see beyond?

3

To see through history, you have to journey back
not so much into time as into self.
Reading, late night, the pages furl past like waves
and you are following the compass point of the imagination.
Scanning centuries, you scry for traces, the glyphs of who you were.
On such journeys, you may sail the coast of a whole era
and not once make landfall. But sometimes, following true north,
you leave the sea, walk inland, then further inland, deep
to the interior of one moment:
Cape Coast. Outside a barracoon. John Newton and an African slaver
haggle over the bowed head of a man kneeling between them.
They do not know him or the trade would end.
But why your feet are stiffening to stone, your mind to ice
as the third man looks up, you know.
The jerk of recognition is a body blow. It doubles you.
And then your feet are raging, your arms are sorrowing out
toward yourself, toward
                              the shock as, eye for eye,
you are stood stock-still by the strange familiar looks of the two men.
Now eye to eye, you recognize
again, and then again, your face.
Which self do you save?

On the journeys inland, you retrace
the inner lineaments of ancestry.
Late night. You close the book
of history.

4

Let them go, gently. All of them: Columbus and his frightened crew of felons;
the Carib warriors of Sauteurs Cliff who leaped to meet themselves;
Hawkins, d'Esnambuc, the swarm of barracuda privateers;
Makandal, Bussa, and all of the enslaved who never became slaves;
the great house masters, the rebels, the informants, the runaways, the
broken at the wheel, the sad infanticidal mothers...
Let them all rest.
Let them fall into a welcoming of sunlit water to a deep, final settling.
Now the loud rodomontade and dazzlingblind dingolay of history's carnival parade
stutters toward silence, dims to a dwindled glimpse
of you closing a book in the frame of a lit window.
Even that will go.
The window blind will draw down like an eyelid closing, leaving
your self in the illumination that discovers you
only in darkness.

AUTO COLONIAL NOTE

Damn! Sold into slavery. Again.
But the buyer is the seller is the slave.
So this time who
will break the chain?

CARIBBEAN MARKET

Seville orange
Ibo yam
Bombay mango
Carib pimento

But who gives a damn?

MT.

This

mountain

has no name. It is

no imitation of Olympus or of Mt. Sinai.

Unnamed, it is more. It is. To know this is to know

i do not know it. And in that weightless moment of unknowing, see.

And it is this seeing, uncalqued by memory, which sears the eyes of history.

HISTORY

Knowing that at the end
Death will acknowledge no identities
i can only half believe
in heroes, villains, histories.

In the clear light of Death
i lower my gaze – I see
shadows, all similar, all
on the ground, haphazardly.

I cannot say which
is Ibo, French, Madrasi, Arawak.
As light climbs, higher,
earth sucks the shadows back.

IDIOETRY

the idiot
goes his own way
speaking an idiom
that he alone at first can understand

the others
pity him   they say
his words are random
no meaning, like scatting, can't be scanned

the idiot
speaks his mind anyway
and sometimes, though seldom,
a few, mad or child minded, answer and

the others
worried over the final say
claim that the idiot is dumb
then they ensure his words are banned

the idiot,
knowing this is the way
that words grow in the kingdom
of language, scats another burst of seeds over the land

BRODSKY

i saw Joseph Brodsky only once
and it was on television —
there was this clip the networks ran
five or six times that day, as they will do.
i don't recall now whom he was speaking to
or when or what was the occasion
but he was making, in absolute seriousness, a proposal
so simple, yet so completely radical,
it could only have arisen in the vision
of a child or poet.
Sow seeds of poetry, he said,
the way the Gideons had done —
a book of poems in every hotel room.

Thinking about it now, three things astound me yet:

how simply one can start a revolution
(my mind's eye saw dark sudden flowers
of poetry everywhere in bloom);

then how the audience, after they'd hesitated,
laughed, as at a celebrity comedian
whose last line was a bit too unexpected;

and how the clip revealed, against its own intention,
that it was not the poet who was dead.

"YOU MAY BE LOOKING AT SOMEONE WHO'S STOPPED WRITING"

For I.D.

poem said, come, let's go for a walk,
but i said, no.
i dread some of those places
you may go

LATELY, THE WORDS

Lately, tasting the fruit of poetry, the words
stick in my mouth, mush, give off a foul odour.
The stink of life is on them.
The grease from politicians' plans,
the mucus of a slickened commerce
thicken in my clogged throat
lately, tasting the words.

It's life, the grey ones tell me;
it has to happen sometime, you have to
join the feast, swallow your early joy
then vomit on your brother.
It always was like this, they say;
if Cain hadn't, Abel would have:
competition, sacrifice.
Somebody has to go.

The grey ones say this,
the dim shapes in the skull's bestiary,
the hanging climbing crawling things
that slough their daytime plastic skins
to slide down prickling nerves at night.
And lately, hearing their chatter and hiss,
i feel their fur, scales, bristles,
stick to my syllables.

And i'm afraid now
that a poem's words, so carefully plucked,
may carry blight, the grey venom of ghouls,
and they may poison you.
Forgive me for this poem.
Lately, the words …

ORIGINS

A black **O**
whole, heavy with the weight
of its own hurt and hungering for being,
feeling within its density a pulse, a moan of light,
the yearn of nothing strending to know itself
in things,
all of the all that time only an **O**,
a closed mouth unclenching, trembling toward declaration:
So
we began.

We are
warm fragments of the substance of sun, meteoroid, far-flung star;
still throbbing in the chest, muted, is the first pain
of the dark **O** splitting heaven-wide open,
shattering into hot shouting light,
agonies ago, long before first aeons, long before
there was a time
or Time.

In time, the spark of word
blazing to a bonfire so we saw
things, saw each other
by the flickering light of language, and all dark beyond.
So
give to the flame, tend to the wavering fire.
All round it, seeping in, the distances, cold,
the black with no sound.
And in our inner galactic darknesses, only the word,
only the bright

O.

AFTERWORD

The words themselves, they vanish, stones into a pond.
It is their ripplings after which disquiet the surface and are seen.
You know their shapes, their soundings, but meaning is beyond
the words themselves, they vanish, stones into a pond.
Moved by the words themselves which pierce us, which have burst through and gone
deep to the self we tremor sentient quiverings straining our uttermost to mean
the words themselves – they vanish, stones into a pond.
It is their ripplings after which disquiet the surface and are seen.

CONTRA DICTION

Since we must hear and see the separate words before the truth they mean
can reach us, there is, always, a contradiction of each word
and the One Word, original, indivisible, which is unheard, unseen.

All words are a translation always from what is to what has been.
Even within the truest poem something was lost, a final meaning blurred,
since we must hear and see the separate words before the truth they mean.

A haze of language shimmering the mindscape hangs a diaphanous screen
so that we see all things through mist and every sound is furred
and the One Word, original, indivisible, is unheard, unseen.

A great poet once, knowing the preterlingual unity of things, tried thirteen
ways to, but could not, translate in poetry the complete perception of a blackbird
since we must hear and see the separate words before the truth they mean.

Yet is it language or the nature of the mind itself which comes between?
And if such division, separation is our essence, what in us is stirred
by the One Word, original, indivisible, which is unheard, unseen?

We are divided. Riven by time, by sense, our first cry is a keen
for a lost wholeness. Our language afterward is an attempt, magnificent, absurd,
to hear and see the separate words before the truth they mean, to reach the One Word,
original, indivisible, unheard, unseen.

CIRCLE OF JOY

For my first drama students

When i first came up here to work in '92,
i had realized an old, old dream: to actually teach theatre.
But so quickly it became something much more, something a lot greater.
i don't know if words can say it. It's all to do with you.

Each one of you. You gave me something,
an unexpected gift, although it probably didn't look that way at all.
You know most classes make the teacher look great, the students small.
To me, we never felt that way. More like a circle, a ring,

like those children's ring games we played all the time,
so simple, so silly, really; yet i can't begin to say
how much these circlings of joy could turn an ordinary day
around, could set my spirit dancing and – look, what i'm

trying to tell you is that you made me, deep down, happy.
And (before we get too damn sentimental here) also fed up, annoyed, frustrated.
But when i review it all, down to the last bow, there was nothing i hated.
Those were two good years. They'll always stay with me.

i still haven't explained just what it is you gave, i realize.
i can't. Something to do with just how naturally you took for granted
that the work must be done well, something about how much you wanted
to improve what you were doing, though there was no reward, no prize

beyond the excellence of doing it well. Believe me, that is becoming rare.
So rare that, before these last two years, I'd started to forget
that people could do difficult things through joy. And then i met
you all, and i remembered. My heart is glad i came here.

Education is coming round to making sense again – and i know why.
Two years with you reminded me that learning and teaching
can never finally be held in theories and grades. It is a reaching
beyond the self you are now to the deeper I.

That's why i have always loved drama – that is something it can do.
And now, in our dancing circle, what i most wish for you
is to meet students like yourselves, who'll learn but teach you too,
who'll give the same gift you gave me, each one of you.

MAMOYI

The child is sleeping,
folded in among the brown boughs of my arms,
and a promise, formed beyond language, drawn upward
like sap through a pith, stirs through me.
In its slow course, i feel a vow so deep
it does not reach the flower and fade of word
but leaves me steeped, resined, in its truth.
Because i wish this child, awake, a man,
to know that he can keep, lifelong,
the trust, the self-astonishing joy that he has now
and he can draw from them the strength to make
his true path from the place i am
to where he will become, for his own child, a tree,
i vow: these boughs will never break.

CREATION

For days, weeks at a time, i lose whatever it is
which keeps my senses softened to the sentience of the earth,
to hillside grass running lightly before a silver wind
or a far slope rippling like a muscled shoulder
or how the gradine, faceted pebbles under me will rasp
as i ease in closer, resting my back
against the rough-skinned body of a gliricidia.

All this can suddenly go without a hint
like a room slips into darkness with a passing cloud –
except, i don't know how,
it happens with no slippage of the sense of self.
On drizzled mornings, when a silver fluttering beats to a white rush down the hills,
i can believe that seraphs bear the rain to us.
By afternoon, wind has lost colour, stones are exactly stones,
the green ascending hill has stiffened into a surveyor's gradient.
The names by which i used to call the earth to come to me
have hardened in my mouth to scabs.

Who was it then who saw the wings of seraphs?
And who is looking now, squinting with eyes of quartz?
i want to understand how, inhabitants of the same life,
they do not know each other, they have never met;
how, looking out of the same windows, they see different worlds.
i want to find a way that they may see each other.
i want them – the glint-eyed one of rationed sight,
        the other, dream-blinded even in the day's light –
to meet and in that meeting learn a threefold vision
that hopefully i may translate into new lines of language,
lines braided from their voices and my own speaking together,
an utterance which, if even for the duration of only a few words,
will speak our earth original again into creation.

THE WILD HORSES OF THE OZARKS

An ordinary weekday, newstime on the television, and the usual:
ethnic violence, unemployment, drug cartels, the homeless,
Dow Jones down again, the NASDAQ falling...

In how many houses were how many people watching,
bleared with information that they could not do a damn thing with
except tell someone else who could not do a damn thing either?

And then, the horses. The network probably saw them as a quirky item,
part of a policy of lightening the news with something quaint.
But no network could have caught them and what they were part of.

The wild horses of the Ozarks – the high-resolution television screen
could only hold them for a moment, then they leaped
out of the frame into whatever they had come from.

And as the news reporter's voice professionally clipped
above a shimmering film of horses almost ghostly in their beauty,
there was an eddying of wind or something in the room.

The park ranger's comment at first was merely puzzling:
"They're strays." But then it rankled. i ended up chasing that word
all week, following it beyond the terrain of my understanding.

Then the word turned round and haunted me toward this poem.
Strays. From where, to where, could such animals stray?
Where, on that part of Earth, would they not be at home?

Within the limits of climate traced in the veins of their own bodies,
within the contours of the natural bourns that all but men inhabit,
what are, what can be, the boundaries of wild horses?

And that was the other word. *Wild.* i would have thought it hackneyed
but the horses stopped all thinking. And the rush that i felt then
was more than feeling. It had the stillness of arrival. They had taken me

to where they came from, where they were returning, they had taken me
to the still wildness we do not remember ourselves to acknowledge.
They had led me, these wild strays, in quiet thundering, to a strange clearing.

i was reminded – no, not true. The truth is, i was re-embodied.
After their hoofbeats faded, i discerned, startlingly near, the dun of my own heart.
The wind that stirred then was the rippling of thought re-entering its flesh.

The Ozarks folk, for their part, had – as they themselves said – horse sense.
They carried placards mocking the common sense of the park ranger,
who, in a way, had strayed from his corralled authority into an unknown land.

They wanted the wild horses left alone. And i praise that now rare wisdom
which allows for the unchartable, sometimes irksome, ways of Earth,
which acknowledges that there must be, too, the uncontrollable.

Wild – syllable upspringing in my throat out of a well of being i can never see.
Word of the almost ultimate beauty bursting the bud of my lips into its utterance.
Wild – name of a land at a forever distance, on the other side of boundary.

Wild horses of the Ozarks, following your thunder i arrive
for a moment where the whole world, remembered, is my body
and I am again the Wild from which it all begins, continually.

Child, listen: Earth is language,
a millioning of words that never needed our translation.
i tell you, if that Man had listened –
Lion roared his name, Rain brought messages from passing clouds,
telling them onto Wind in chattling green tongues
all over the garden. Nothing was dumb. All spoke.
They didn't need his names.
He thought they did.
That's how It began.

The rumour going round is that it was Snake.
Not so.
Snake was his brother, why would Snake do that?
Snake tried to make him see
what he was doing. Naming the earth! For what?
Earth had named him.
All he had to do was listen.
If he had listened, he could still
have called them, spoken to them, spoken to All.
But with their own names, the names they gave
themselves, talking Earth language.

But not him. He never even heard his own.
Too dam' busy –
naming. Translating, really.
Now he don't even know his own name. Up to today.
i believe that's why he talks so much. Trying to find out.
And worse, he lies.
When Snake got vex and called him a dam' fool,
he didn't like that. Well, who would?
But when the Woman asked
what Snake had called him, he said:
"A dam'—"
and couldn't bring himself to say the rest.

That was the first lie:
that his name was Adam.
He never learned his own name,
his true name – in Earth language.
Yet Earth is nothing else but language.
A millioning of words that keeps on talking to you all the time.
So, child, whenever it is you wake up,
listen:
you may hear your name.

BROKEN BOWL

To integrate the fragments of the self into a whole
is the only real task. But that's easy to say.
To do it is the work of lifetimes – and there's no one way.
Like when you're reassembling the pieces of a broken bowl,
the sequence of that depends upon what fragment you first take.
After that, shard by shard, trial and error, attentiveness
unto the shape forming itself under your hands. Nonetheless,
even the shards themselves sometimes will fall and break.

And then you have to start again. But do you, really?
It wasn't you who broke the bowl, it always was in fragments.
The self, when you first know enough to know it, is already
shattered. Yet something moves us to restore this delicate faience
because we know, when we have made it whole,
we can hold all, even the sun in water in a bowl.

HURRICANE

Fanatic, reeling in a dervish dance,
grappling at trees, mountains, homes, the other rooted things,
flailing away surfaces, trying to clutch beginnings,
only desperate for stillness, for a godlike glance
that will absolve this rage into a larger whole,
reveal – if even afterward – that there is some meaning
to these walls broken, fences uprooted, the people leaning
on each other, some naked almost, from the sudden cold,
the hurricane wields its violence by accident,
straining to reach an absence at the centre,
chasing a vision hidden in the chaos,
and that restless searching always brings a havoc to us
till a god's eye, seeing our hard-set fences shatter,

acknowledges this driven heretic a saint.

THE DOGS

It's evening; this elegant, coiffured New Yorker walks her three dogs,
or they walk her. True, each well-groomed beast is on a leash,
but, quivering with instinct, they dart, stop suddenly, sniff, rush
off where they choose, dragging the lady with fierce tugs.
Park Avenue madam, but she has no choice. She has to follow them.
The Chanel clothes and Christian Dior face she wears are suave
but make no difference; sophistication never has made dogs behave.
They piss and – damn, they've bolted. She calls, but they don't come.

Embarrassed, she misunderstands my smile. She cannot see or hear
my pack of dogs that all day, panting, haul and tug me.
i am leashed lifelong to obscure hungerings, a hairy urge to roam
the dark streets of the self, bolt from the avenues' bright glare.
And just sometimes the thought comes (as to her now, i see):
What if, following the dogs one evening, i lose the way home?

SANE BLUES

Oh i've tried for long to be sane
And now i'm trying to see my gain
i wonder
i wonder

For years i've kept myself held tight
I must have thought that this was right
No longer
No longer

'Cause i'm losing the reasons for holding it in
Perhaps i should let go, let my self give in
to this hunger
this hunger

Suppose i let that self run loose?
Would it run to a bible? A woman? A noose?
i wonder
i wonder

Blue sky? Black cloud? Win or lose?
How can i know? How do i choose?
. . .
i hear thunder

QUAY

Contrary to history,
Columbus made one voyage only, the very first.
The rest were trips.
True voyages begin in faith, in desperation, a last hope.
You have to go: the flatness and inertia of your world
are levelling you down to a slow, blank death.
You have to go: even the society's guarding dragons –
    sly curling sneer of cool derision
    the eyes of ice that freeze the ostracized and isolate heart
    bared grinning iron teeth of barred gates
    the dark vertiginous throat of welcoming insanity –
seem no worse than this unliving without end.
You have to go
although the only guideline is to go too far.

Columbus, standing at the quay,
wondering at the border of firm land and the unsettled dreamwide sea...
How often had he done this? How often you? Stand at the edge,
rehearsing – but you can't – a journey without maps.
What do you leave? To what do you return? Do you?

It is a death, it cannot be rehearsed, it is a death
and it will separate you: from the stranger in the mirror,
from your failing words falling always to another grey floor,
from the actions and the destinations of a half-life where your self is not.
It is a death, this voyage,
this crossing to a latitude no one can measure.

But if you find safe passage
through straits of mind-narrowing fear,
the weary deadcalms of horizonless despair,
round a blind headland somewhere past hope,
there will be a birth.
This is the faith. The last hope.

BRIGHT

Consider this:
that death may not be
a darkness, but a white light so harsh
we have to close our eyes.

See it then
as an illumination that we cannot face,
a lucence that we turn our backs against,
fearful of blindness.

And yet we know
the wavering shapes before our squinted eyes
are not quite true, they change too much
although we name them down.

Consider too,
though not with blind belief, the rumours
of the few who, opening their eyes to seering light,
saw without shadows.

Perhaps whether death is
a darkness or a light finally depends on how you see
things. Sometimes when you really see a thing
in time, knowing it must go, it can seem so bright.

LIGHT

For Margaret Gill

and with no trumpet call or tongues of flame
you are remembering the times of the miraculous
you are remembering a remnant of people at a bus stop
standing as in a shaft of light
itself within the wide undifferentiating light of Wednesday afternoon
you are remembering
that weekday moment rippling outward with no effort
into – not past and future though it is tempting to describe it in that way, but –
something which is both and neither
a long continuous eddying outward taking every thing into itself till it is everything
and you inside a passing minivan
your mind a null in the daze of objects blurring toward you
until that moment
you are remembering now

LIKE WIND

Hardest to understand
is that here too there are seasons:
times of the harrowing of spirit, the dry days of no hope,
the Lenten times when everything is fallow, waiting for the grace of rain.
To understand this is to know
that dying is a season also.
And knowing this you rest in the integrity of the unhandled world,
the manifest inexhaustibility of things, how trees keep dying into fruit,
how fruit keep dying into trees again without complaint,
how there is, always, earth.
But that understanding is a season also, is a grace.
It comes like wind, like wind you cannot grasp it.
And if in its visitation, for the lived duration of a moment,
you see that everything – grass, lilies, the least hair on your head –
is moved by that same breath,
give thanks.

ABOUT THE AUTHOR

Born in St. Lucia in 1952, he studied and lived in Jamaica in the 1970s, where he explored his talents as a poet, playwright and director. As a poet, his writing ranges across the continuum of language from Standard English to the varieties of Caribbean English and he has also written poems in Kweyol, his nation language. He works in traditional forms like the sonnet and villanelle as well as in so-called free verse and in forms influenced by rap and reggae. He has published five books of poetry and his poetry has appeared in various journals such as *The Greenfield Review*, *The Massachusetts Review* and in anthologies such as *Caribbean Poetry Now*, *Voiceprint*, *West Indian Poetry* and others. He has also edited *Confluence: Nine St. Lucian Poets*, *So Much Poetry in We People*, an anthology of performance poetry from the Eastern Caribbean, *This Poem-Worthy Place*, an anthology of poems from Bermuda, as well as student anthologies from creative writing students at the Sir Arthur Lewis Community College where he was a lecturer in literature and drama until 2007.

He has participated in poetry workshops by Derek Walcott and Mervyn Morris. He has himself designed and taught poetry workshops in various places such as Ty Newydd in Wales and the UWI Caribbean Writers Summer Workshop in Barbados.

He has performed his work in the Caribbean, Europe and America at events such as the Miami International Book Fair, the Medellin Poetry Festival, Calabash Literary Festival, Vibrations Caraibes, the Havana Book Fair among others. In 2007, he won the Bridget Jones Travel Award to travel to England to present his one-man dramatized poetry production, Kinky Blues, at the annual conference of the Society for Caribbean Studies. He has twice won the Literature prize in the Minvielle & Chastanet Fine Arts Awards, for many years the premier arts award scheme in St. Lucia. He has been the recipient of a James Michener Fellowship to study poetry and an OAS scholarship to study theatre. In 2012 he won the NGC Bocas Poetry Prize for *Fault Lines*.

He has also established himself as an innovative playwright and director, authoring eight plays, and directing scores of others, including his own *The Drum-Maker* (1976), *The Song of One* (1995) and *Triptych* (2000), all of which have been published in drama anthologies. In 1984, he co-founded the Lighthouse Theatre Company in St. Lucia, and has long been involved in all aspects of the dramatic arts on the island. He has toured with theatre productions in the Caribbean and the UK. At different times he has been involved as actor, director and administrator in Saint Lucia's contingents travelling to CARIFESTA. He is an original and continuing member of the syllabus panel for the Caribbean Examinations Council (CXC) Theatre Arts programme and serves as an external examiner.

In 2000, Kendel was awarded the St. Lucia Medal of Merit (Gold) for Contribution to the Arts. Recently retired from the Sir Arthur Lewis Community College, his present focus is to use his skills as a writer and dramatist to raise public awareness and contribute to active solutions of critical social issues.

ALSO BY KENDEL HIPPOLYTE

Birthright
ISBN: 9780948833939; pp. 124; pub. February 1997; price: £8.99.

The Heinemann Book of Caribbean Poetry described Kendel Hippolyte as "perhaps the outstanding Caribbean poet of his generation". Until now his poetry has only been available in anthologies and slim collections which have been little seen outside St. Lucia. *Birthright* reveals him as a poet who combines acute intelligence and passion, a barbed wit and lyrical tenderness.

He writes with satirical anger from the perspective of an island marginalised by the international money markets in a prophetic voice whose ancestry is Blake, Whitman and Lawrence, married to the contemporary influences of reggae, rastafarian word-play and a dread cosmology. He writes, too, with an acute control of formal structures, of sound, rhythm and rhyme – there are sonnets and even a villanelle – but like "Bunny Wailer flailing Apollyon with a single song", his poetry has "a deepdown spiritual chanting rising upfull-I". Whilst acknowledging a debt of influence and admiration to his fellow St. Lucian, Derek Walcott, Kendel Hippolyte's poetry has a direct force which is in the best sense a corrective to Walcott's tendency to romanticise the St. Lucian landscape and people.

Kwame Dawes writes: "It is clear that Hippolyte's social consciousness is subordinated to his fascination with words, with the poetics of language, and so in the end we are left with a sense of having taken a journey with a poet who loves the musicality of his words. His more overtly craft conscious neo-formalist pieces are deft, efficient and never strained. Villanelles, sonnets and interesting rhyming verse show his discipline and the quiet concentration of a poet who does not write for the rat race of the publishing world, but for himself. One gets the sense of a writer working in a laboratory patiently, waiting for the right image to come, and then placing it there only when it comes. This calm, this devotion is enviable for frenetic writers like myself who act as if there is a death wish on our heads or a promise of early passing. Our poetry, one suspects, suffers. Hippolyte shows no such anxiety and the result is verse of remarkable grace and beauty."

Fault Lines
ISBN: 9781845231914; pp. 76; pub. 2012; price: £9.99.

If you want to feel what it's like to live on a small island, vulnerable to the wounded thrashings of world capitalism in crisis, an island where livelihoods are destroyed at the flourish of a Brussel's bureaucrat's pen, where Paradise is a tourist cruise ship come to remind you of your neo-colonial status, where global consumerism has poisoned the ambitions of the young into drugs, crime and violence, then the poems in *Fault Lines*, dread, urgent prophecies of "a black sky beyond" are indispensable guides. With the verbal urgency of Ginsberg's *Howl*, a visionary imagination that shares the company of Blake, *Fault Lines* confirms Kendel Hippolyte's reputation as one of the Caribbean's most important poets. What he does so brilliantly is catch in the same poem both a precision of observation and the indeterminacy of the observing mind, the awareness that "whatever drove us was also banishing/what we were driven to". And there is not only that kind of doubleness, but the stunning ability to create poems that appear to observe themselves in their moment of creation, like "Silverfish" with its radical truth that "the secret all empires must suppress, in order, to metastasize into empires" is:

at the I-magination lives beyond our ordering and is our ordering.
nd a true poem is a glimpsed oblique track opened by the strenuous silver writhing
    of a poet
riddling a living way through dying language, creating a whole, hoping we fall, mindful,
    into it

MORE POETRY FROM ST LUCIA

John Robert Lee
Elemental: New and Selected Poems
ISBN: 9781845230623, pp. 120; 2008; £8.99

John Robert Lee brings a quiet, reflective, often autobiographical approach to his concerns with Caribbean life, art and faith. Within carefully crafted formal structures – and some experimentation with traditional forms – he finds the space to give his voice and persona free rein. Whilst rooted in St. Lucia and Caribbean culture, he takes the whole world as his arena – as much at home writing about Boston as Castries.

Undoubtedly the foremost Caribbean Christian writer of his generation, his is a truly incarnational view of faith, anchored in the reality of human experience and expressed in richly textured images of Caribbean landscapes, dress, street life, music, dance and his native Creole language.

Jane King
Performance Anxiety
ISBN: 9781845232306, pp. 122; 2013; £8.99

"Jane King" is very much present in these poems, though never in obvious autobiographical ways. She is the observant eye taking in the beauties and droughts, climatic and human, she sees in St Lucia and in the semi-public lives of her neighbours. Hers is also the inward eye that plumbs dream states, the unconscious and the alarming darkness that the free-floating imagination sometimes reaches.

Vladimir Lucien
Sounding Ground
ISBN: 9781845232399, pp. 64; May 2014; £8.99

Vladimir Lucien's poetry is intelligent, musical, gritty in observation, graceful in method. You can see a young man building his house of poetry, just as his poems reflect on building a marriage and making his home, and all the accommodations this demands. He builds his house with stories of ancestors, immediate family and the history embedded in his language choices as a St Lucian writer.

All available from Peepaltreepress.com with safe on-line ordering and at cost or below carriage.